THE MUSIC OF THE SOUL'S GIVE AND TAKE

Selected poems by
Anne Gruenberg
2022–2024

Edited by Kelly Davis

Photography by Clare Park

Published by Francis and Davis Editorial Services

First published 2025

Photograph of Anne on p. 42 taken by Karl Gruenberg

A modified image of the Sagittarius dwarf irregular galaxy from the Hubble Space Telescope. NASA, ESA, and The Hubble Heritage Team (STScI/AURA) appears on p. 64.
With thanks to Paolo Tozzi, astronomer at INAF Osservatorio Astrofisico di Arcetri.

Book design by Russell Holden, www.pixeltweakspublications.com

ISBN: 978-1-913898-92-2

A catalogue record for this book is available from the British Library.

Front cover Image: *Night Drum* by Amanda Ravetz

For Margaret, my sons Ben and Gabriel, and my grandchildren

Contents

Editor's Note

This poetry collection continues the story begun in *A Square Foot of Sky: a reawakening in words and images, 2019–2021*, after Anne Gruenberg's incarceration in a high-security prison in 2008 and the thirteen years she spent thereafter in psychiatric institutions and care homes. That book ended on an optimistic note, with Anne gaining her Absolute Discharge in August 2021.

We all want stories to end happily – and Anne's friends and family hoped she would find some peace. But sometimes, especially for those living with mental and physical disabilities, the pattern is 'relapse and resume'. In late 2024, at the time of writing, Anne continues to experience depression and complex post-traumatic stress disorder. She is also bed-bound, due to an incurable degenerative spinal condition. Her only in-person contact is with staff members and occasional visitors.

Recently Anne has been emailing her poems to a small group of friends: Brendan Hughes, Susie Barson, Christine Meldal, Clare Park, Debbie Green and me. They flowed in a torrent (sometimes three or four a day) until 31st October 2024, when she told us she was finding it too difficult to write and she would no longer send us poems. We decided to end the book at that point, even though Anne will no doubt continue writing, as she says it 'quietens the demons' in her mind. When Anne previously had relapses, we sometimes feared we might lose her. We have always tried to carry her in a web of love. That web requires her courage, and our affection, to remain unbroken.

Anne has written these poems, with great difficulty, on her mobile phone. They have given her a lifeline and a means of communicating with the world. As a fellow poet and a professional editor, I have selected representative poems from her prolific output over the past two years.

In *A Square Foot of Sky*, each poem was only identified by the date on which it was written. This time, I felt they needed individual titles, which I have chosen. I have known Anne since we were five years old. We have much in common, including our Jewish heritage.

Her father, a maths professor, left Vienna on the Kindertransport in 1939. My mother's father escaped from Lithuania, where his family died in the Holocaust. And we each have two sons.

Many of Anne's poems speak of spiritual matters and have a translucent beauty; others are written in darker moods, expressing deep anger, regret and grief. Certain images appear repeatedly, and there are references to real experiences in the care home and to Anne's earlier life, as a child, daughter, teenager, dancer and theatre designer. She is also the mother of two adult sons (Ben and Gabriel) and now a grandmother. These family relationships, mainly conducted via Facebook Messenger, are central to her existence.

She has asked us to publish these poems. They shed light on her journey and her inner life. We hope readers will find them as moving as we do.

Kelly Davis
www.kellydavis.co.uk

Photographer's Note

As a photographer there is a big difference between being part of the action and being a witness to the action. With Anne I am not an onlooker; she engages with my camera and what we create together sometimes starts a bigger conversation.

During the 1990s we made some powerful imagery about what life threw up during that time but latterly the images expressed something of the pressure Anne was facing within her family life. She became the subject and storyteller of her own traumas through the expressivity of her body, until her creativity sadly ebbed away over two decades.

From 2008 I remained in contact with Anne whilst she was in hospital, until we met again in 2019. During the Covid pandemic a creative collaboration developed between me and two other long-standing friends of Anne, Kelly Davis and Debbie Green. A book of poems and photographs, *A Square Foot of Sky: a reawakening in words and images 2019–2021*, was born. (See Appendix for further details of this book.)

Since then, I have continued to photograph Anne from time to time and we have shared many light-hearted moments together. The impromptu portraits reveal not only Anne's beguiling presence but also her vulnerability. The imagery derives from our shared backgrounds in theatre and dance, and motherhood.

On 4th November 2024 I spent four hours with Anne and departed with very mixed emotions and an enormous yet familiar sense of helplessness. Over the past two years, she has undergone annual relapses – and it seemed the pattern might be about to repeat. I spoke openly to her about what I observed and what I thought might help.

Huge physiological benefits could be gained from leaving her room, after spending a whole year in bed. I left feeling there was an outside chance that she might agree to be supported in moving from her bed to a wheelchair, despite the initial pain it might cause her.

Throughout the relapses and returns, we have remained Anne's constant and loyal friends, and her family give her joy and a purpose in life. I have encouraged her to prompt me with ideas for photographs to sit alongside this new poetry collection. We exchange all sorts of cultural delights between our friendship group and much of Anne's inspiration comes from poet Mary Oliver, artist Andrew Wyeth, writer Wendell Berry, singer/songwriter Patti Smith and poet John O'Donohue.

On 20th November a photograph of Anne sitting outdoors in her wheelchair unexpectedly arrived by text. I was surprised and delighted that she had had the courage to brave the move from her room, despite her daily life remaining fragile and uncertain. Anne once again left her bed when I returned on the vivid autumnal day of 29th November. We made some new portraits capturing the essence of that memorable afternoon in the garden, until the sunlight dipped behind the trees.

Clare Park
www.clarepark.com

RETURN
May to November 2022

Anne visited her son Gabriel and his partner in Thailand in Spring 2022. While she was there, her mobility improved, and she was able to enjoy swimming and sailing. When she returned to the UK, she moved into 'a house for vulnerable women' in Heston, West London.

Goodbye or au revoir

Goodbye to all those walls
all the voices I heard
the alarm bells ringing
all the despair I saw
the boxes of nappies
and endless cups of tea
to the untameable spirit of youth
that dragged me from the mire
and put me back on solid ground.

Goodbye to the stone slabs
in the courtyard
goodbye to the buttercups pushing
delicately between them
giving nature a chance
the hungry birds
that brightened my days
the lilac tree
outside my window.

Goodbye or maybe au revoir.
Like the beast
I am shedding more scales
as kindness rescues me
from the darkness
from myself.

The brightness of my room

Welcome to the metal birds
roaring through the skies
the skinny cat that I secretly feed

the whiteness
the brightness
of my room

the wanting to be cleansed by the rain
by a warm shower
with room to dance
but tiles to slip on

the open faces
I will come to trust
unlike my balance.

New beginnings
or have I just come full circle
to the place
I once knew?

Learning
as if for the first time
that not every outstretched hand
will strike me down.

Does the grass feel different to a free woman?

Do the clouds still cover
the noonday sun?
Is the robin's song sweeter,
the rose more fragile?

Arms held out
in ceaseless embracing.
Love, the prize
in all our beginnings
and endings.

How does a bed feel
to a free woman?
The hot water of a shower
on her back?
The joyous singing
of the congregation
as one body.

Promises made
and promises kept
as all that is holy
is laid in front of her.

Suspended

The tree with blossom
the scent of orange has gone
the cats have gone
and cigarette smoke
lingers in the rooms.

I slip between weekly changed sheets
and you continue to visit me
in the dead of night
when the robin is quiet
the sun shining
on a different part of the earth.

And my heart is vulnerable
and bruised
yet my grandmother's smile
appears sometimes
on my face.

Then dawn breaks
and fear comes,
as constant a friend
as my morning coffee,
and I search for that peace
between words.

As light fills the green shadows
of distant trees, painting the rose
a vermilion red,
I understand everything has its place
and I find myself
suspended from the clouds
while a little piece of the dancer
falls to earth.

A trip on the kerb

There aren't that many precipices in Heston.
The nearest you can get to falling
is a trip on the kerb

Grief traces her manicured fingers
in the skies above
with jet trails weaving
in
out
and beyond

As constant as your love for the birds
the trees
the meandering stream
the heaving ocean

But just as you are ready
to step in front of the curtain
grief hits you like a freight train

The nightingale's throat

My name bleeds
from the wounds in my chest,
from the breeze coming through
an open door,
rides on the backs of gulls
and sits high in the sky
like the noonday sun.

It is wise to step back
into the valley of tears,
eventually meeting the other side
of a dark chasm
that has formed
at my feet
and named itself life.

My happiness is strung
about the throat
of the nightingale.

The long dark arm of night

Did you see the pigeons
and the red admiral butterfly
and the red kite swooping

when sirens and landing planes filled the air
and I fought for air in my bed

seeing the long dark arm of night
stretching before me

when children were quiet
but the neighbourhood dogs took over
as I attempted to make my mind the sky.

Good intentions

The weight of the ceiling
the weight of your good intentions
the weight of the night sky
pregnant with the sound of questioning
half listening
half floating
like feathers
on the edge of sleep
or death.

Piranesi on the iPad

And the Piranesi emanating from the iPad
and the dappled evening light on next door's pebbledash
and the sun blinding me –
and painting the folds of my duvet
like a mountain range –
could be construed as something holy.

RELAPSE
November to December 2022

After refusing food and medication for some time, Anne was moved to a mental health unit in a hospital, under a 28-day section.

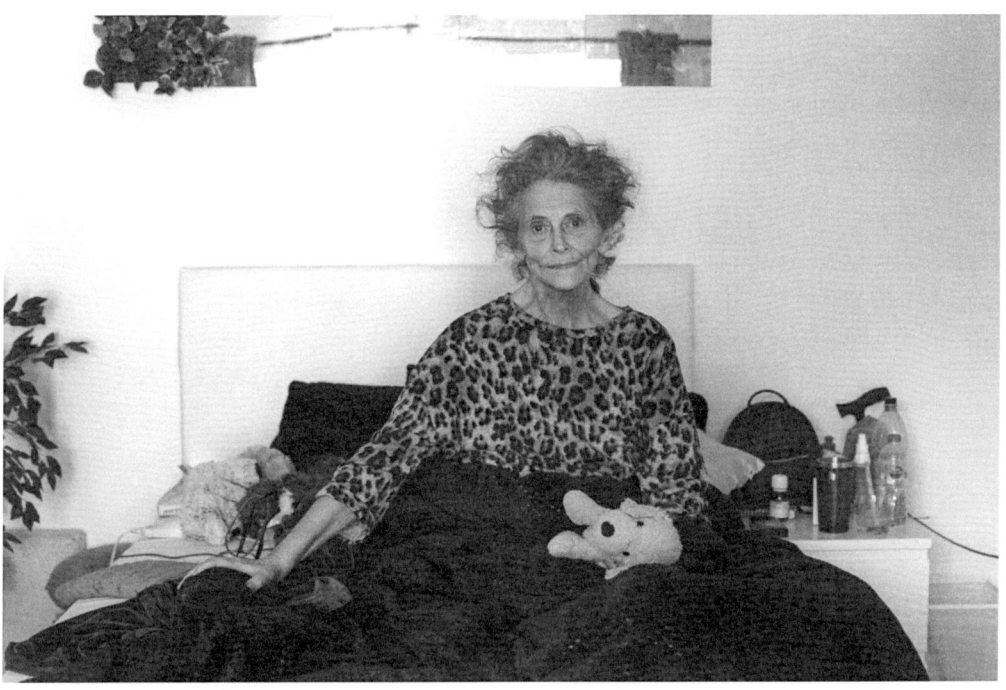

Sleep no more

Drip drip goes the IV fluid into my arm
Drip drip goes my soul onto the non-slip hospital floor

Unseen for years
Caught in the web of others' wishes and judgements
I don't think they know that I have already left this earth
So am doomed to sleep no more

To imagine Maggie Hambling's wave paintings
To imagine an English woodland
A seagull's feather blown in a winter breeze
A rocky outcrop
A perfect pebble
To imagine being held in the arms of unconditional love

In the sky

They did not know I was not here
The footprint on the kitchen tiles
The stains on bathroom towels
The presence as stealthy as a fox
Eyes glowing in the moonlight

You did not know I was not there
But for the moving of plates
The changing of shirts
The whispering of promises

I never said you would see me in the sky
But when the heron flew by
I left the summer lawns and joined her

Oh, I see a square foot of sky again

The leaves brushing the cloudscape again
The fake wood floor
The hand on the door
The uniformed care about the corridors
Scrabble and flowers on the table
Reflections on the walls

My despair bound up
somewhere above my head
which contains nothing
but old photographs
and unfriendly rollercoasters
that rise in the dead of night

And oh Lord my soul
in disarray
like the bottom
of a concubine's drawer

And I know now
that the wounded
will always carry
the wounded

Why do I feel nothing?

I understand the message of the Lord
but it doesn't resonate through my body,
from my matted hair
to my fingernails.

Am I really still alive
or just a container
for nothingness?
A shallow grave
an empty memory
a box full of dust
where glittering sunlight once lingered

Not allowed

The trees beyond the window whispered
of acceptance and connection
with something universal
and oh so personal.

But we're not allowed to go there,
even though a bench beckoned
in the amber road illumination
and the fallen leaves were like
a fairy forest's carpeted floor.

So I sat by that window
in the unnatural heat,
where my mind left
its black and white memories –
my father always at arm's length
amongst reams of paper
that spelled out my future.

And I heard the sounds
of a generation disturbed
by dissolving terrors
as my body retreated
into the wheelchair.

Beauty is sometimes elusive

The curve of your son's cheek
and his shy smile
that reminds you
of the gangly disobedient adolescent
skittering and erudite
despite the prolonged silence.

Grown-up now,
hair flecked with grey
and a healthy non-addictive lifestyle,
brought close through Facebook Messenger.
Speech unnecessary,
not aware of the wild skies at sunset.

The view from my hospital room

To contemplate mountains,
blue, grey and pink, at dawn,
from my hospital room,
their presence dispelling
all whys and what ifs.

Longing for their steadfast energy
to suffuse my sheets
in the peace of forests,
the energy of rivers tumbling into the sea,
salmon jumping upstream.

Tears don't flow
but the pain is as real
as my need for the air
of moorlands and clifftops.

I found a feather on my bedside table

I had been away a long time,
long enough for me to forget that feather.

But I didn't forget its significance,
and realised that it would always be a sign.

What of, I cannot be sure.
But it would be gentler

than I had dreamed before
or would dream again.

RESUME
December 2022 to August 2023

On 22 December 2022 Anne moved back to the 'house for vulnerable women' in Heston. She was moved to a newly built room at the end of the back garden, as she had requested. She could see her bird feeder there and spend time outside.

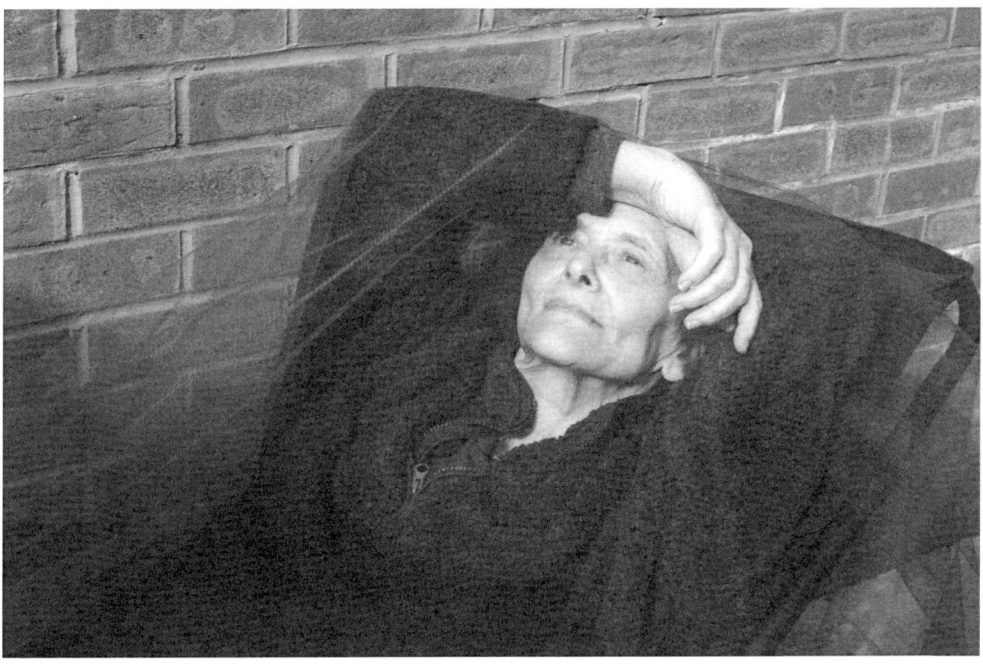

A badger in its sett

I used to find the smallest spaces to curl up in,
like a badger in its sett,
a nightjar in her nest,
before anger and fear caught my vertebrae
and laid me flat.

I wanted to be like the baby
inside the Virgin Mary's womb
reaching out
to pick cherries from the tree.

Now, struggling to breathe,
I long to relax into the depths of night,
a receptacle, a space
where it's alright
to say I can't.

Where am I?

I'm not in the house
for vulnerable women in Heston.
I'm not in my previous partner's home
where salmon and champagne flowed
with unaffordable laughter
and forced merriment.

Nor in my childhood home, with the once-a-year
homemade Christmas cake,
cold linoleum floors and the palpable lack of a father
which led me to curl up in the smallest spaces,
waiting for him to emerge,
though he is long gone –
a plaque displaying all that was felt but never voiced.

Now the voile curtains blow
through the open window
and through a soul that yearns to be free
as the kestrel on the moor,
unstifled by central heating
and the bars on my bed.
I long to see the stars
as O'Keefe did from her rooftop.

A half-remembered time

The angles of the next-door rooftops break
into a heavy January sky
like the sharp edges of my brain
that longs to tell my body
to move with a grace
I once took for granted.

Now there are unseen bolts
in my neck
that hold me rigid
as a telegraph pole.

Are we all just numbers?
Or are we the wind
that rustles through the branches
of the old oak tree,
the seashells indented in the sand,
a half-remembered time
when freedom was a given?

Not there

I seemed alight
But I was not there

I seemed to smile
But I was not there

I shuffled along an unforgiving floor
that held past mistakes
But I was not there

They took blood
and attached a drip to my bruised arm
But I had long gone

I held you in my arms
But I was not there

I watched the birds swoop and float in the sky
and I felt closer to the trees in the forest
But you still didn't know I was not there

Don't weep for me when I leave this mortal plane
because I always loved everything that sang

The choice

What was I supposed to do?
Ignore the mysteries of a mind awakened
and take the medication prescribed by those
who had forgotten how to run
free and wild in forests?
Or watch the deepening orange
of a sunset and ignore
the chattering in my head,
becoming so still and quiet
that the dawn chorus sang every day
through my bones.

A million sorrows

The echoes of birds
on a morning of January frost
and thawed feelings

Oh, I want my tears to fall like April rain
alighting in concentric circles
in puddles on the streets

Waiting for the crocuses
among the icicles and snow
and a million sorrows

And all those who have gone before
to return, so I can wish them
a safe journey to a place I know all too well
where the air is no longer of value

And the dance exists
only in minds
not in limbs

Unsullied

White folds all colours into itself.
Time whittles away minutes, days,
weeks, years.

If we become too afraid to look
we won't see the white shining
through everything.

From clouds in the sky
to freshly laid turtles' eggs,
from snow on fields
to swans on a lake.

From the candles continually burning
in the temples of the faithful
to an untouched artist's canvas
waiting on an easel.

A meanness of the heart

I begin to see the breadth and form of it –
of my washroom,
of the pebble-dashed house
at the end of the green grass,
of my sadness.

Am I like the deer peeping out
from behind a tree,
still unsure of its place on this earth
and without a mother
to guide it?

No shooting stars
no exploding fireworks,
just the stillness of an English winter's day
the ever-present birdsong
and a silent small meanness of the heart
that grows like hemlock
on motorway verges.

Daily list

No need to achieve anything anymore,
apart from uncurling my fingers
so they wrap around yours.

My daily list includes:
eat, breathe, breathe again
and notice the ballerina pink blossom
on the trees in next door's garden.

Remembering reaching towards the sky
like those trees,
saying nothing at all.

A truth beyond words
in hearts that are now soil
and roots that interlock
like fingers in the earth.

Falling in love with pain

Curtains blow in and out
with my breath.
The promise of a new day
then a sliver of afternoon light
like the dance of clouds across the sun.

When will this nausea subside?
The sound of rushing water on the iPad
reminds me what it is like to get up.

To be surrounded by air
to stand with feet in the earth
head in the sky.

To want only what I have,
to fall in love with the pain,
the ever-changing light on the sea
as it breathes in and out.

I wish to be the wind

I'm so lucky to see the sky,
to watch clouds embracing one another
in an endless stream of mutuality.
They are a backdrop for the birds
and a witness to my tears.

The sky is a blanket for my pain
a place where I glimpse
the gentle watchman
the mystery
the pathway to eternity.

I wish to be the wind,
to stand on a cliff
and not be afraid,
to find some peace there.

I gave everything to charity

I was left with Yo Yo Ma
and chocolate ganache,
a view out of the window
of trees and sky.

I wanted to be as light
as a Buddhist nun,
as the bird who flies above my head
the fox who runs beneath the moon
the stag that groans on the moor.

But I hadn't considered
the weight of memory
the weight of loss.

RELAPSE
September 2023 to December 2023

By September 2023 Anne was no longer communicating with us. She refused medication and stopped eating. The 'home for vulnerable women' could no longer provide care for her. In November 2023 she was sectioned once again.

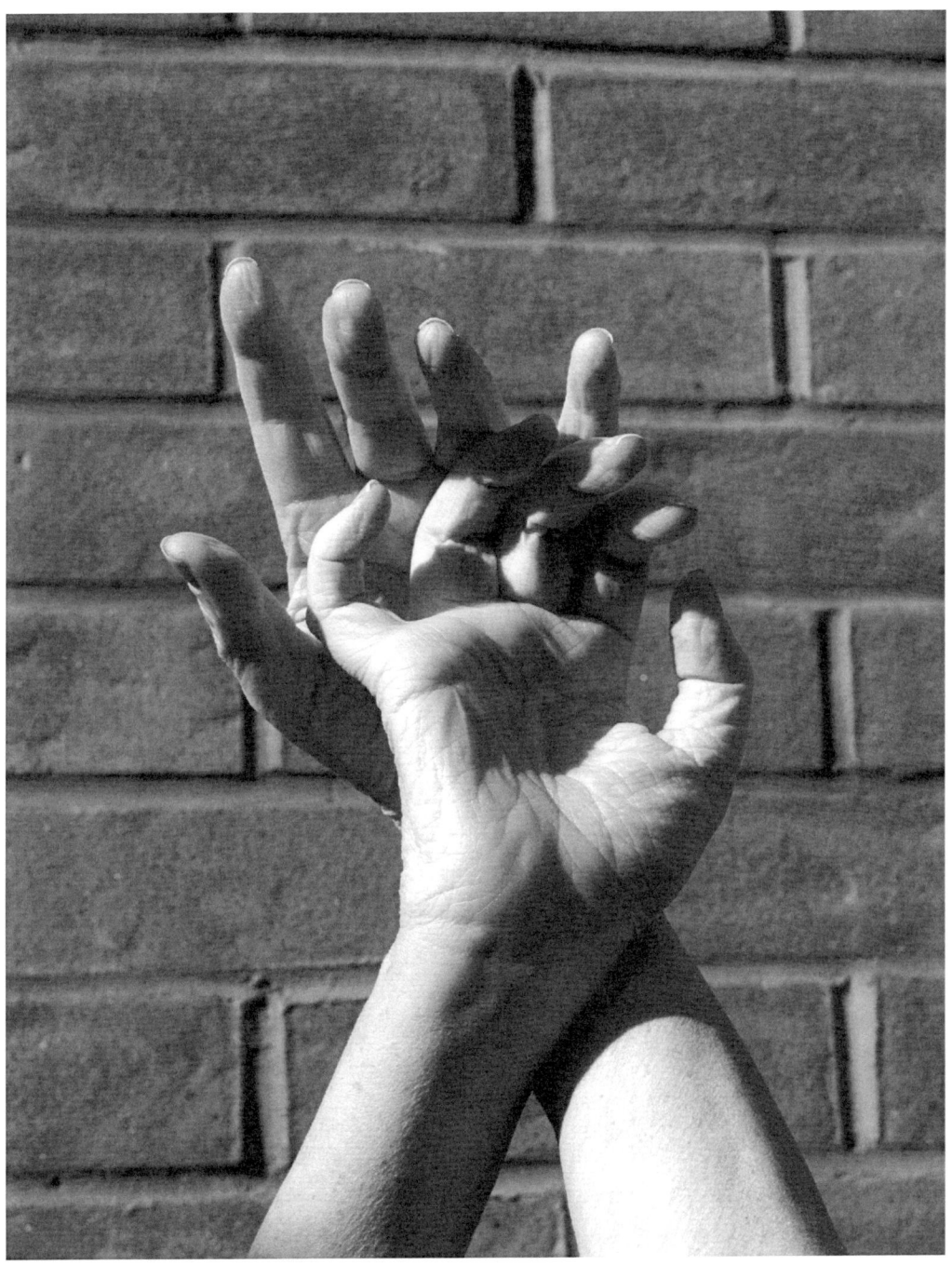

When I can't contain this grief any longer

I turn to the poet's verses
the linden tree
the swan.

Making a furrow
in this plane of sorrow
for everything lost
in the sea of love.

Swirling silently
and finding a shore
on which to finally rest
in the beauty of it all.

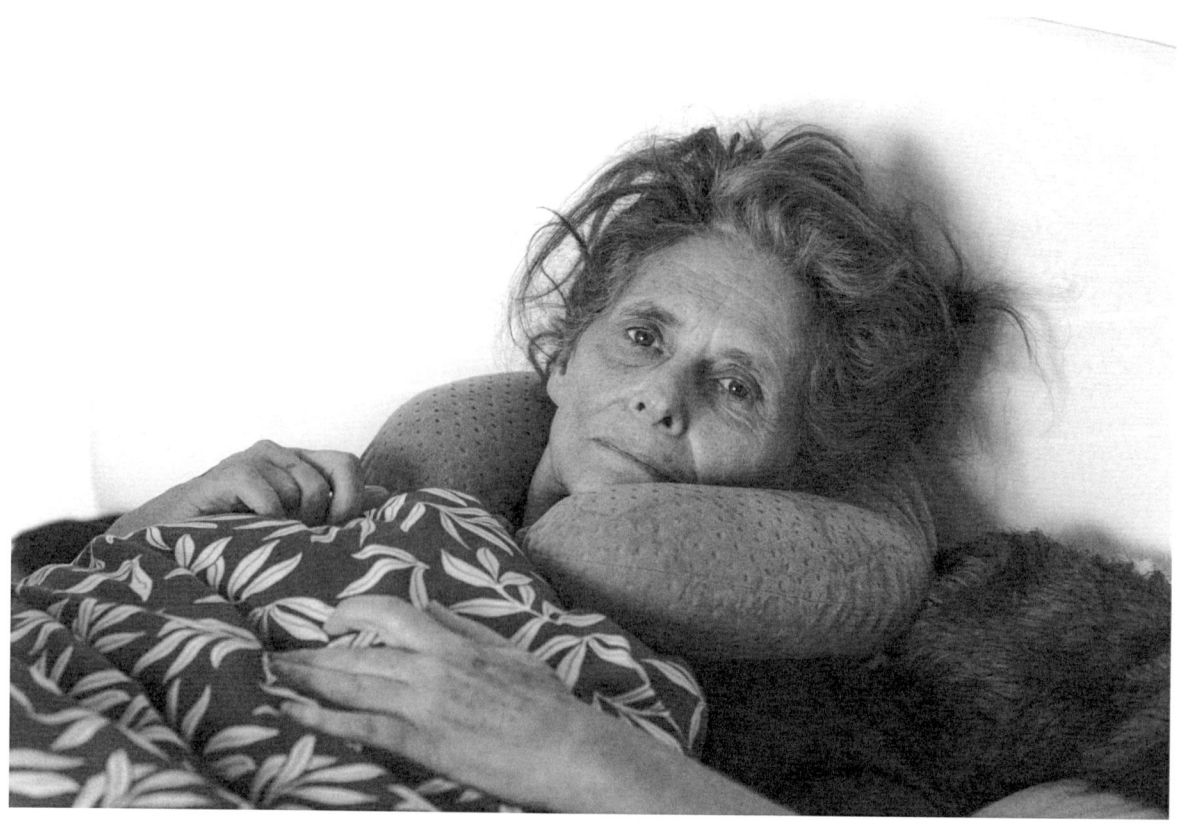

Words have so often eluded me

When my father left
this mortal plane too soon
a cry from somewhere deep down
left through my mouth.

When you were in the hospital
I smoked cigarettes
and buried my head
in the steering wheel.

I watch the swans
lift themselves into the air.
Grace so fleeting.

Safe

Last night my hummingbird lantern
made me feel safe
for the first time I can remember.

No harsh lights
no television noise.

Only the buzzing of bees
the blueberry bush
the dying honeysuckle
by my side.

And the slowly dawning skies.

Soft within my heart

The sea doesn't know
that I think about her
all the time

Whether she's moving in or out,
her subtle breathing
caresses my face
as I watch the net curtains
caught on the morning winds

And the leaves on the little fig tree
hugging their lime greenness
smiling at the wavering grass

That everlasting carpet
soft beneath my feet
soft within my heart

When the night spirits take hold

Just me and the neighbour's black and white cat
and someone's car alarm
up at 4.30am
when the night spirits take hold
and I wrestle with them
between tears and coffee.

For a minute the world
stops turning
and I sit alone
in this naked place
staring at the pink flowers
painted on my cup.

And then it's daylight
and dandelion clocks
and butterflies
dance their merry dance
in front of my eyes.

The sky is always there

'Find a little crevice somewhere,'
a friend said,
'and look at the sky.'

Among the pickles and pastries
I buy strawberries
along the bumpy pavements
past the roar of urban traffic.

In the local park
I look at the purple flower
in my hand
as a flock of pigeons
take flight.

Ladies of a certain age
giggling
gossiping
stroll by.

And clouds gather overhead.
The sky is always there.

A letting go

I want to empty myself out
onto a blank page
and while the night enfolds me
in her velvet arms
feel a letting go.

The smell of the garden
wafts in through the open door,
reminding me of fields
and my young heart's enthusiasm
to run.

An open sky
turns towards me,
her hands
holding out
all the stars
in the galaxy.

Animal time

I live in animal time.
No clocks, no weeks or months,
only dark and light.

I have just one dream –
to feel love
in this broken body.

Niagara of memories

And I know the love that leaves us
never truly leaves.
But still I cover my eyes with age-spotted hands
as if to stem the Niagara of memories.

While the pigeons fight voraciously for bird seed
and I shop for spring bulbs,
as if I might engage in their beauty from the bed
that has become a trap for rats, spiders and jam.

Sometimes words are just pebbles thrown into a lake.
Silent but we know they are still there, in the depths,
waiting to guide us home.

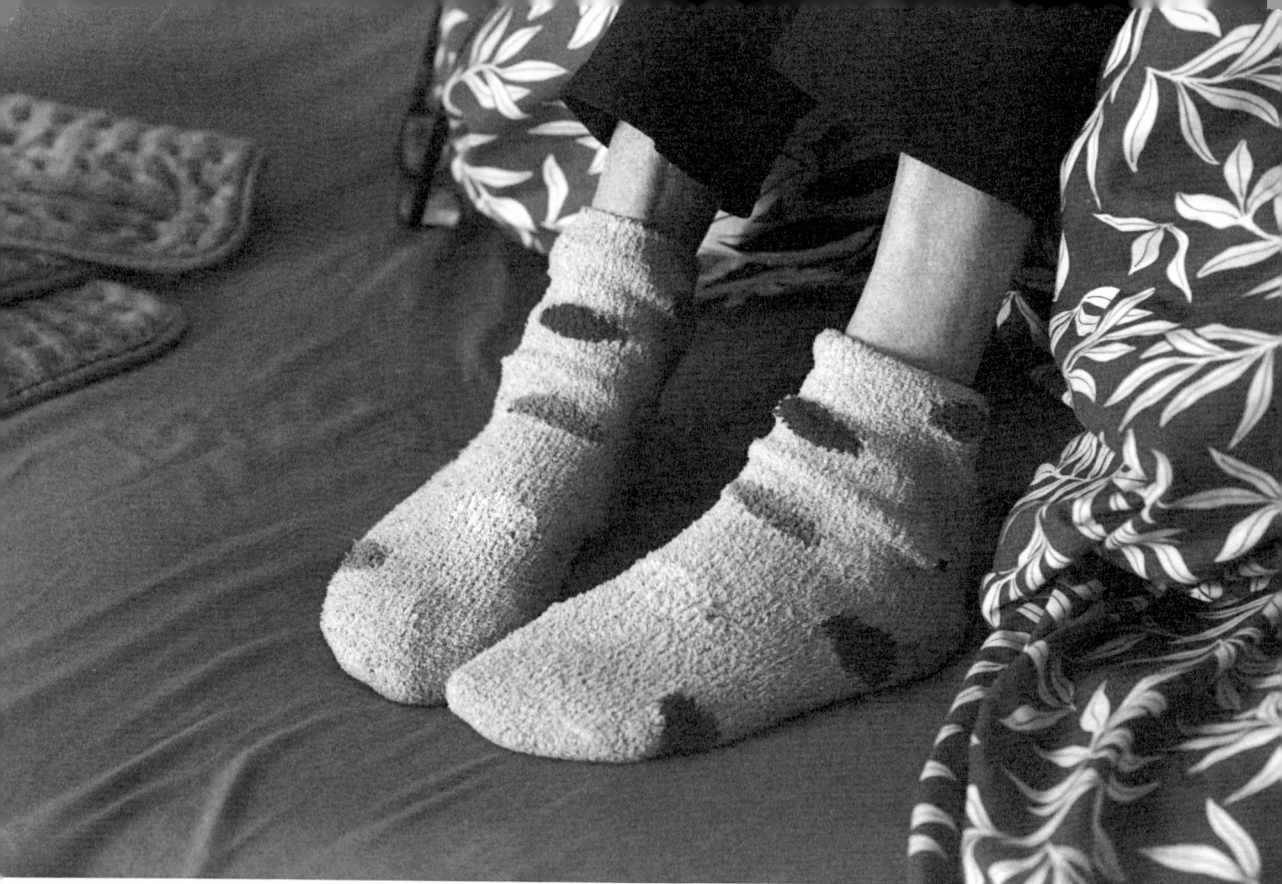

Something nurtured

Do I see mountains
or is it just the net curtains
on the windows
at the edge of night?

Do I see Mary weeping
at Christ's feet?
Or is it just the recycling bins
by the back wall?

Every day the sky lightens
but my heart remains
rooted in the unforgiving ground
where fresh green shoots
miraculously appear.

As if air from the mountains
has breathed life into
something nurtured.

A deathly quiet

Behind every joy
there is a deathly quiet,
the silence of trees
on the path to the housing estate
and the berries too high to reach.

The back turned,
of someone you love.

And still the music goes on,
like the swirl of water
in the trunks of ancient oaks.

The dappled light of love
crosses oceans,
flies above the disintegrating clouds
and lands in meadows of ragwort and poppies,
spanning centuries
and waking you at 3am.

Planting mint

Love and loss hang in the air
like a curl of smoke
from a long-ago late-night bar.
And I wonder if I should plant that mint.

There is another world
inside this one.

A vertical drop into experience
where exposed laughter
and tears linger
in parallel worlds.
So the decision to plant out the mint is made.

And the early bird singing
speaks of life
just because.

And another dawn is anticipated,
as is the incoming flight
from Sydney, Australia.

And the scent of lovage
lingers on my fingertips.

Open to the sun

What do you feel
when the lilac flowers
of the hosta
no longer shimmer?

When a pair of gulls chattering in the cloud-heavy skies
remind you of winter storms at sea,
and the thought of another day fills you with the fear
that flows from open palms
resting on rumpled sheets?

Look at the rose blooms in the pot
and remind yourself
of your grandson, his face
open to the sun.

RESUME
January 2024 to October 2024

In January 2024 Anne moved into a residential care home in Hounslow, where she receives 24-hour care.

The mask

I am so glued to the mask
that people respond to that
and not my fluttering dying inner world.

Children, ex-lovers, friends
all communicate with me
as if I were a walking talking human being.
But I learnt early on at school
that the mask was attractive
and if I showed just a fraction of my dented soul
I would be vilified,
thrown to the apocryphal wolves.

Today I'm not sure if it is me
or the medication –
the dark pools in my eye sockets,
the drowning, the falling down,
the self that likes pistachio halva
or the self that wants to cry a thousand tears
and lie down forever
beneath ancient oaks,
cradled at last
in the arms of the earth.

Who knows our hearts?

I lay my doggy hot water bottle
on my tummy.
I've never owned a dog
but this is as close as I can get
to finding comfort.
My breath is stuck behind my eyes
as I struggle not to panic.

Trying to believe that all is well
and that the nausea that surges up
is not the result of you
but my inability to get to the truth.
Like the infectious calm
and beauty of my carer
as she wipes me clean.
Who knows her heart?
Who knows mine?

If there is time

I am constantly met with the mundane
The cleaner with her bleach
The carer coming to change me
Talking about the weather endlessly
checking on Google if they are right

The sun breaking through the clouds
The hot water bottle
heavy on my chest
Another cup of tea
two bags please

The sight of you on Facebook Messenger
too far away
The tears that threaten to cause a tsunami
One door shutting
Perhaps another opening
if there is time

Flowers regal and motionless
in their vase

39

Why do I keep my curtains closed?

Maybe because the great hand of God
might pluck me from my bed
and drag me through the streets
of this West London borough
with takeaway leaflets
and barbed wire
and mystery

Oh I remember beauty
but she sometimes eludes me,
though she remains shining through
everything, even creeping round
the edges of my curtains
reminding me there is no end
just continuous beginnings

Seagull eyes

I looked for a smiling face
but all I got was concrete and wood

Seagull eyes
nightmares at midday
barefoot in my bed
running away
from the inevitable
riding the waves
as they ebb and flow

Bones creaking
as I sip tea

The headphone lead
coiled around my neck
like so much razor wire

Twilight

Was that my mother
sitting beneath the tree,
my father on a ladder
to the stars?
And was I crawling between the two
with little rabbit feet?

Falling in love with twilight
in a hospital bed,
my dreams lying
in tatters on the earth,
magic swirling like honeybees
around me.

A flawless line

Last summer I saw a sick cygnet
on the lake, beneath the willow,
reflected in the water,
just as the leaves were
saying farewell to summer,
their crimson and russet tones
setting the air alight.

I would have donned waders
to rescue him,
I would have brought him inside
to be healed,
but I was in a wheelchair,
being sick myself.
So I watched as his mother
led his siblings upstream
in a flawless line
and I prayed for that little creature
who didn't know what a perfect circle was.

A riderless carousel

It's all gathered in one circle
and my mouth is feeling bent and wrong
as I manoeuvre a biscuit
towards my face.
A face coloured with such longevity,
a face I cannot see or own,
taps where the eyes should be.
My forehead painted and warm
like a riderless carousel.
I want to breathe the sky
not rainwater from the gutters.

Driving in his car

I was a slip of a girl
but I danced like a soul possessed.
I lost all sense of time and place
on the dance floor.

When a person of the opposite sex
approached me
in the flashing disco lights
and asked if he could take pictures of me
no it wasn't vanity
but an intense stupidity
which made me agree.

When we drove in his car,
I knew not where,
a creeping sense of panic
began to wrap itself around my throat
and I became very quiet
like a baby bird
fallen from its nest.

And when he asked me
to take my top off
I was almost paralysed with fear.
Nothing untoward happened
but I remember the terror
like it was yesterday.

My mother put
one of the clothed photos
on her wall.

Art makes everything beautiful

I had my nails cut today.
A routine act, you may think,
but the cutter was a young man from Kerala,
never met before.
And so I unburdened my checkered past,
well, some of it,
to this gentle young man
with eyes like a doe
who said that art
makes everything beautiful.

One eye on the sky

Shall I meet my eleven-year-old self
at the funeral pyre?
She who loved to run, loved sunny days and the rain?
Oh, but she saw her feet as she was dragged mute
up the stairs to a room
which would never again be her refuge.

She heard her mother's muffled tears
and the attacker was gone.
But so was her childhood.
The muse had now left her
as she ran into her future,
one eye on the sky.

What is really happening

If I wrote down
what is really happening
in my head I would scare myself.

And I can't walk alone to dissipate
such negative miserable thoughts,
the sky looking down on me in disgust.

I would like to swing through the trees
better now than I have ever been.
But it may not always be so.

I need to change my life.

I want moments of radiance

Like the sun on a summer's day
the roses in the vase
my grandson's ebullient laugh
the chapel at Mass.

But they disappear into the night
where everything is formless.
And there is nothing
in the written word
to explain the chaos.

A garden

I lie in this bed
not talking, not walking,
barely conscious.

But I search for God every day,
knowing his gentle touch
and his wide open heart.

He will make a garden of my life,
taking fear away from my body,
because I can't fall anymore.

A bag of crackers

The act of folding
a bag of crackers
focuses my mind.

I don't have much to fold,
being bed-bound.
But maybe one bag of crackers is enough.

Like those women from a bygone age,
whose husbands and sons were at sea,
where icebergs form and stormy winds blow

I can send out the only thing I know,
which is love.

I'm just waiting for something to happen

In this darkness, this void,
where bone crunches against bone

In this silence
I hear a petal drop from the vase

The afternoon sun describes
the form of the tree outside

swaying in the breeze
Oh, to hear the window fidget at its fastenings

as though I were at sea,
the music of the soul's give and take

Flying

Warbling like a songbird,
the soprano sings across the airwaves,
reaching into my skin and bones.
I am hoping to be lost in that magic.

To fly as free as our mothers told us we would.
Before that tragic fall one Saturday night
out in the suburbs, without a hand to hold.

It's all coming home to roost,
as they say.
And I am only a tiny piece
of the story.

Snowballs

A tiny dog twists and turns
in freshly laid snow.

I remember a time
in a pine forest
when I threw freshly made snowballs
at my brother,
my lovely papa looking on.

I was safe and free.
Now all I have
is the cleaner's mango disinfectant
to remind me where my loved ones are

and billowing clouds
outside my window
to remind me where I am.

Love goes to waste

Are there any nightingales left in England?
I came across one in a children's book,
her presence an indelible memory.
She literally sang her heart out
for love of a rose.

The same love I have for this chaotic world.

And this love goes to waste
in the recycling bin,
the heat of this summer's day
filling my degenerating senses.
A smile so easily worn away.

Too quiet

'It's feeling autumnal today,'
you say.

'I'm so very lonely and in so much pain,'
are the words you can't communicate.

'Is there anything else you need?'
as he puts the coffee down on the table.

'No, I'm fine,' you lie.

I exist two feet above my body
and wonder if I'll ever come back to earth.

Like the sky
I've been too quiet.

Birds own nothing

That's why they can fly.

I gave away all my clothes
as I have no need of them,
being in bed.

I gave away all my books
because I have
no concentration.

I have only my loved ones
behind my eyes – and memories,
some good some bad.

While I wait for God to give the word,
I watch imaginary swans flying
in perfect alignment with my breath.

Falling is not the problem

The sweetest of words
has the bitterest taste.

This is a gift from swollen rain clouds
and moody landscapes.

Falling is not the problem.

It's hitting the ground
that makes the whole world change.

Prayer

Dear God, you hold my heart
in the palm of your hand

and then you turn it over
to reveal all the songbirds
of the world

showing me the way
through wind and rain
on the darkest night

in my room,
which could be a cathedral,
where I speak through the silence
wondering if anyone can hear me

Music is found sound

waiting for the ether
to pluck it up miles away
and drop it at your feet

stress, the necessary grit of life,
can be washed away with a few cello chords

notes suspended in air,
so light it feels as if an angel
were standing at your side,
sun reflecting off his wings

A red grapefruit

I can't make the hills
or the hot Mediterranean sun.

But I need to remember
that my love

is a cool mountain stream
or the heat of molten lava

as sweet as lavender
as deep as the ravine

as constant as the bird's song
shining through a poet's mist

scrabbling about to find kindness
on this earth

And then I remember
I've got a red grapefruit in the fridge
and no one to share it with.

A longing for wings

Awakening beneath the dark
a further adventure awaits us –
one of the heart.

Like a flower that opens in the daylight hours,
finding the moon as it lights our nights,
so that all the colours assemble
to take leave of the day.

And the heart grows still –
awakening the young soul for a new tomorrow,
where time has become the circle of eternity,
where there is no loneliness or shame.

Truth and love no longer distanced,
someone has filled the cup for us,
as we return to the home we left
before memory formed.

Roses

The roses in my vase
are like flowery nectarines
or raspberry-ripple ice cream.

And there are acres of rose bushes –
I have forgotten where
but I can recall their intoxicating scent
as if I were lying beneath them
at this very moment.

I'm always surprised that every year
they lift their heads to the sun,
giving us so much joy.

And with autumn coming we bring them inside, and
put them in a vase, to remind us of how the summers felt
when we were carefree and holy.

Monastic heart

When you find love
the shy air around you is clearer
the rain softer

And you relish the solitude
because you know you are not alone

And you can listen deeply to the night
without drowning

And even though you sit alone in your cell
your love touches the world

And the sky reaches down
to scatter it over those who are lost

Looking for the song

When I was up to my mother's knee
movement was a God-given joy.

But I didn't realise it – until it had gone
in a split second.

And I crawled through my life
to the place I'm in now.

Crashed on my bed,
bone crunching against bone,
looking for the song.

Intimate sounds

I had decided not to write anymore
but then I heard a Philip Glass etude
and I had to communicate
what it made me feel.

Open and unobtrusive

with a longing to fly over closed spaces
and the haunting melody of memories
the intimate sounds of light and truth
the pathos of a cavernous world.

Kintsugi

The desire to love is opening
opening into the abyss
and filling it with gold

Gold that mends cracks
gold that shines out from above
even on the darkest winter's day

It is in the towel discarded on the floor
and in the trees, as their branches bow down
as if in prayer.

How can I become the actress in the play?

I could only move to the dictates of notes,
could only emote
with the words written down.
Was it a trap or a release?

And will I turn into the flower girl
at the wedding, holding the love
for someone else?

Hoping for showers
so I can dance once again in the rain,
in that freedom the spirit cries out for,
a minute before passing into another realm,
with pictures of trees in my mind's eye.

RETREAT

October and November 2024

As autumn changed to winter, Anne began her retreat, sending a final flurry of poems.

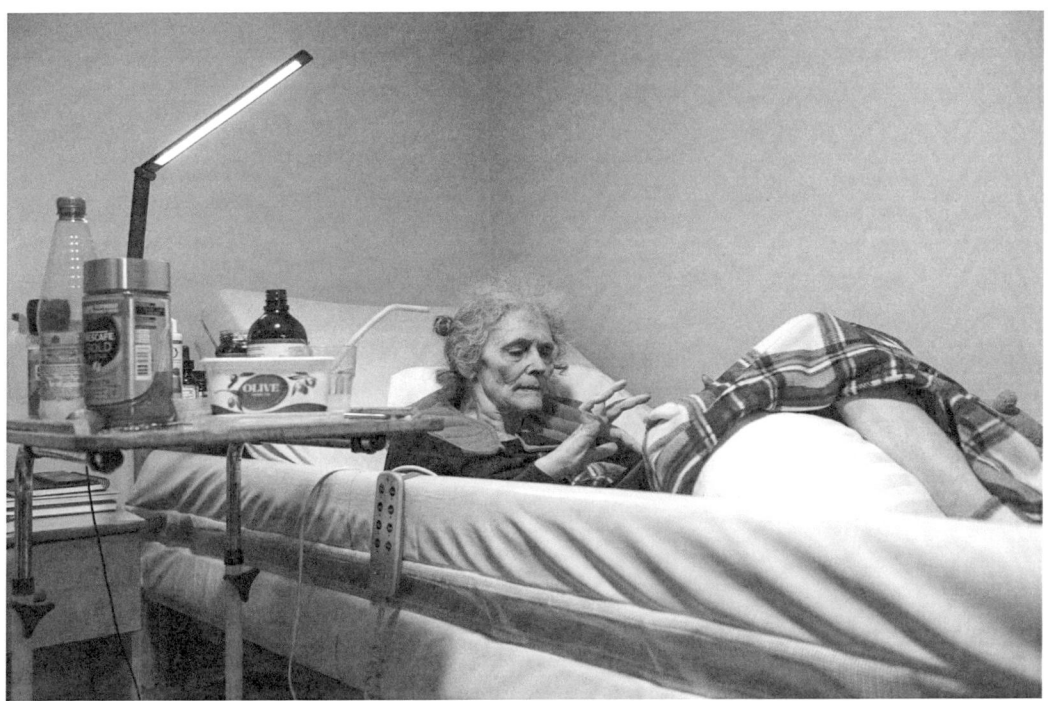

It's raining again

And the window mists up.
Is the sky weeping?
The trees bow
as if in supplication
to a cloud-heavy sky.

I'm not so thankful.
The bells keep ringing,
reminding me that I'm not in the forest
and my anger has no one to play with
so I might as well make friends with the pain.

A random bee

buzzed past my window.
Does he not know what season this is?

The leaves are certainly aware
as they turn red and brown
and slide slowly to the earth.

Where do the bees go in these changing times?
They will return to pollinate
summer's bounty next year,
under the dream of blue sky
when all the birds sing yes.

A breath away

Oh, I want to wrap my arms around you.
I look at the clock and time moves so slowly –
tick tock tick tock.
You are both a breath and a lifetime away.

I would steal myself into the walled garden
where everything makes sense –
overblown crimson poppies growing for you
the beech tree hugging the earth
stone cherubim looking heavenward
herons bowing their heads at the water's edge
golden carp hiding beneath lily pads.

In a stillness like a churchyard
in a silence like the grave
or like my room.

I believe I live in a poem

Some are built of steel
some flow like water
and some disappear into thin air.

A poem is a gift to the living
not the dead,
though they may take some
beyond the grave.

A poem can come up to meet you
when you lose something irreplaceable
or detonate that brick wall
you haven't got the strength to climb.

It is like the silence between chords.
It can be an explosion of colours
like a sunset
or the starry mantle of night.

It is a leap of faith,
a broken resurrection.

Did your angel have glass wings?

Did they break one day,
shattering the sun's brightness,
when you fell into endless night?

When you were lost
in the darkness of suburbia
with those who couldn't see you
or the choices you made,
out of melancholy, or the mania
nibbling at your mind.

'Oh she's ok,
just stunned.'
And I was frozen for years,
running away in my sleep
without knowing it.

Oh yes, my angel had glass wings,
though I didn't see them shatter.
I was the thunderstorm
by the back door.

A memory of swans

I imagine the warm embrace
of another. I felt it once
but now it's just a distant memory.

Like swans in the air,
their beating wings
sounding like a holy sigh
from beyond the clouds.

For a moment nothing else matters.
The memory is a lament
as endless as a mountain stream
rushing down to the ocean.

World view

My daddy took us to see
the Angel Glacier in Canada.
It was magical.
Ice like outstretched wings
glinting in the morning sun.

They say it has shrunk conspicuously.
And I would like to be sure
that my grandson will visit it
and change his view of the world
so he will look for angels everywhere.

Eyes full of pebbles

What do we find beautiful?
Is it the pebbles on the beach
Is it the distance in your eyes
Is it the leaves as they come tumbling down
or the river as it rises?

Maybe it's the way your nose creases up
when you laugh?
And you laugh all the time.
The world is a happy place for you –
not for you the snakes and eels
of my existence.

The sun colours the sky
with aching beauty each day
just for you.
Just the spaces between words
just open joy
to be in that skin and those bones
that rival the sun.

Death knitting by your bed

There is a reality
but you don't remember it.
You are nothing, yet also everything.
Don't give in to appearances.
You are loving awareness.
It seeps from your fingertips
it flows over your brow.

One morning you will wake up
to find Death sitting by your bed.
He is knitting, and he never finishes.
You've found crocheting too difficult
but you have watched him
with his needles
on many a lonely night.

The song may be over
but the cantata has just begun.

Those who have gone before us

Where is the candle
that lights us to bed
and scares the ghosts
hovering over us?

Those who have gone before
but still hold us captive
with their silent howls
their perpetual tapping
on the door of consciousness.

Making each day
a journey down a dusty road
that leads nowhere,
the sun illuminating
these faltering steps
these silent howls
in this beautiful shatter-able place.

As night lets down its curtain

The birds fly into the sky as one
and the trees outside begin to whisper
and the plants in my room begin to sing
and I feel life slowly slipping through my fingers.

Though I still feel the beauty
of the flowers in the vase,
and there's a deep forgiveness in my heart,
I don't catch the rope before I fall.

The brightest flowers

Shall I just sit with it?
This nothingness
This empty cargo
This lover of tea
and you.

Everything we want
is a dream away
while music plays
in distant lands
and birds sing
on the wing
over oceans and continents.

And the clatter of cans
in the recycling bin
of my life
is heard
like the hum of a honeybee,
doing what bees do –
landing on the brightest flowers.

A final poem

A whoosh of November air
rushed through the doors
and onto me

Even in the enclosed courtyard
I felt a little freedom
a little relief

The grass was still green
and I was able
to breathe a little deeper

Afterword

Anne says:

'These are poems written, usually in the moment,

under increasing degeneration of my body and mind.

Loneliness and solitude have become my bedmates.

The act of writing quietens the demons in my mind.

This book therefore ends with no ending.'

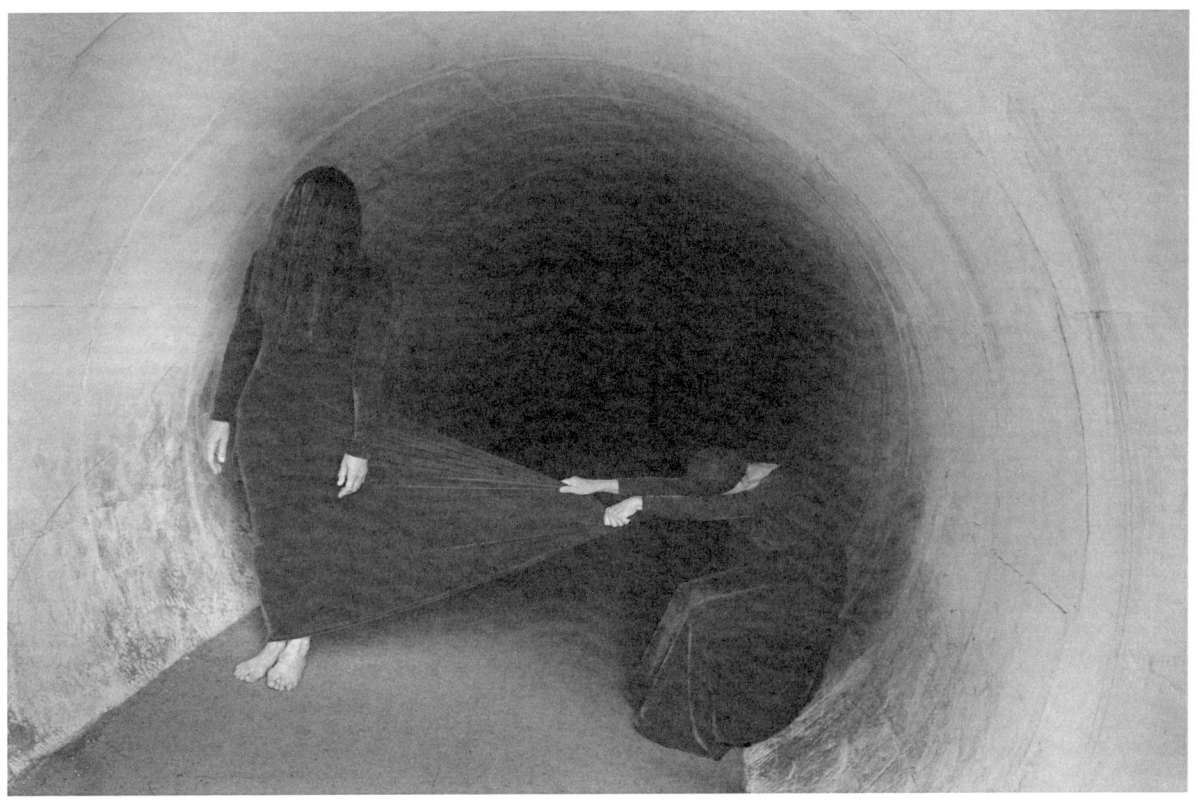

Response by Amanda Ravetz, artist

I am caught in the throat. It's Clare's photograph of Kelly catching a handful of Anne's hair. It whips me back into an intense research project I did with children in a nursery class in 2019. I am sitting in the heat of June in a sandpit with my three-year-old classmates who are running their hands through my hair and asking 'is this your baby hair?'

Kelly, Anne and I share personal history. We were at the same school from age 11. The two of them already had a bond as flexible, strong and delicate as spider's silk. That web, which extended to other friends, and over time included photographer Clare, is evident throughout this book. It is in Clare's images, Kelly's editorial care and of course Anne's poems where it is sometimes radiant and glistening, at others sticky and broken. But it is a web that matters not just to those of us who know Anne, but to anyone who has experienced love and loss.

As I read Anne's poems I am plunged into moments of great darkness and great beauty. The first section deals with themes that ripple on through the collection – the wounded psyche with its hesitancy, its desire to trust. *Have we come full circle or is this a new beginning?* they ask. Alongside the poems, Clare's photographs capture the delicacy, fragility and hopefulness of new life. It is early summer in this first cycle of 'Return'. After a spring in Thailand with family, Anne sits on the bed leaning towards Clare, towards us the viewers, with her hips fully opened. In the next image though, she has turned inward, perched like a bird on an old-fashioned upholstered armchair, her hips closed, her eyes shut against intrusion. A wind chime hangs inside a closed window with what I imagine is an absence of sound. Freedom, with its possibilities, its expectations and its demands, has a Janus face.

Anne is missing her grandson on the other side of the world. Separated from her own innocence, here is the come down. Freedom, it turns out, is just a suburban street – so where is the vitality of life which just a few moments ago was felt coursing through the body and the breath?

She sits behind the veil of the curtain. How to recover, how to redeem all the scarred scared torn splintered and split-off parts? The night is a 'long dark arm', when the sharp focus of sunlight and shadow relaxes, and stark opposites bleed into each other.

All this is held within the rooms of bland routine and well-intended institutions – net curtains, pebbledash, heavy ceilings, fake wood, slippery tiles, unnatural heat, away from which the mind flies, has its escape, its fantasy. Seeing mountain ranges...

Then 'Relapse'. Thinned and diluted, flown, the body in the photograph merely a mirage. The poems tell us: *you think I am here, but I'm gone, high on dreams.*

What do we feel when we read about this experience of care that tends to the body but not the soul? For me it is the pain of impasse when the soul has done a runner (or ascended) from the hygienic tick tock of time, dissociated so as to float away on a grey mist where the body's imprisonment is just an idea, an abstraction, a frozen lake over which Anne is hovering like the kestrel in her dreams.

Full of dissociation on the one hand – all the poems about not being in her body – and transcendent beauty and grace on the other. This is an exquisite study of the psyche's oscillations, sometimes cradled or swallowed by darkness, at other times levitated within light.

Amanda Ravetz
www.amandaravetz.co.uk

Appendix: *A Square Foot of Sky*

Designed by Matilda Cicely and published in 2022, this book combines photographs with poetic dispatches from a world that few of us can imagine. Anne Gruenberg was incarcerated in 2008 and spent thirteen years in psychiatric institutions. Having experienced extreme isolation, depression and chronic post-traumatic stress disorder, and now with limited mobility, one might expect her story to be unremittingly tragic. Yet she has found a voice.

Written over a two-year period within the confines of her room, Anne's poems take the reader on a journey from breakdown and despair to reconnection and redemption. Even when she could only see a square foot of sky, she could see birds. And that made her feel there was still life – and hope.

Fellow collaborators and long-standing friends of Anne, photographer Clare Park and dancer Debbie Green, have interpreted her poems visually. The performative photographs are a response to Anne's poetry through a shared language of theatre. As The Dancer moves through different landscapes, the poems and images 'speak' to each other through the pages of the book.

'A work of magnificence. Moving, poignant, enraging and, yes, hopeful.'
Susie Orbach – psychotherapist, psychoanalyst, writer and social critic

To find out more about this unique publication, please visit:
www.clarepark.com/asquarefootofsky

To order copies, email: clareparkphoto@hotmail.com

www.ingramcontent.com/pod-product-compliance
Ingram Content Group UK Ltd.
Pitfield, Milton Keynes, MK11 3LW, UK
UKRC030014010325
455715UK00003B/17